Quick & Fun

Writing Activities
Just for Young Learners

Easy Writing Lessons with Reproducible Graphic Organizers
That Teach 26 Different Kinds of Writing

By Martin Lee and Marcia Miller

Writing Is Fun!

S C H O L A S T I C
PROFESSIONAL BOOKS

New York ☼ Toronto ☼ London ☼ Auckland ☼ Sydney

Mexico City ☼ New Delhi ☼ Hong Kong

To Liz, Chris, and Jeff;
to Amanda and Brody;
and, of course,
to their terrific parents

Cover design by Norma Ortiz
Cover illustration by Nadine Bernard Westcott
Interior design by Grafica, Inc.
Interior illustration by Maxie Chambliss

ISBN: 0-439-17033-8

Copyright © 2001 by Martin Lee and Marcia Miller. Published by Scholastic, Inc.

Printed in the U.S.A.

Contents

Contents

About This Book

How do you inspire young students to write? You present a variety of ideas that are appealing and authentic to spark their interest, curiosity, and playfulness. You provide engaging pre-writing activities to make children think about ideas they will genuinely want to write about. You offer writing aids—graphic organizers, clearly designed forms, useful checklists, visual cues, or themed stationery—that enhance creativity and organization. *Quick & Fun Writing Activities Just for Young Learners* combines these approaches to inspire children to write.

The 26 activities in this book present opportunities for children to try descriptive writing, expository writing, creative writing, persuasive writing, narrative writing, and real-world or practical writing. Because our target audience is primary-level students whose writing skills may be rudimentary, the activities are simple, clear, and easy to use. Every activity begins with one page for you, the teacher, to help you guide the way.

You will find the same basic lesson plan for each activity.

Get Ready . . . offers pre-writing activities to whet the appetites of young writers. Do one or two, or try them all.

Get Set . . . tells you exactly how to focus children on the specific task at hand. It explains which pages in the book to duplicate.

Write! is self-explanatory—it's time for children to put pencil to paper and go for it!

Get Together gives ideas for presenting, publishing, and extending the activity.

For each activity, one or more reproducible pages written to children follows the teacher page. Directions are brief but clear. A quick glance will tell you how children should use these pages. Many of the activities are open-ended; you can adapt them to your classroom as you wish. As a bonus, look at the section **More Writing Ideas From A to Z** on pages 84-85. These ideas appear as titles for activities, but we envision that they will stimulate your creativity as a writing teacher.

At the back of the book, you will find a Self-Evaluation Checklist, a basic set of Editor's Marks, and four different certificates you may present to young writers as the circumstances dictate.

We hope that *Quick & Fun Writing Activities Just for Young Learners* will help you guide your students to experiment with writing and luxuriate in its many possibilities. The activities will motivate children to think about audience, purpose, voice, tone, language, and meaning in age-appropriate ways. We want the writing activities to entice young writers to dream, think, draw, plan, imagine, question, explain, clarify, and, ultimately, to communicate. In the process, we hope they will develop a genuine sense of pleasure, confidence, and accomplishment as emerging authors.

Bon voyage to you and your class as you embark on a joyous journey into writing.

Martin Lee and
Marcia Miller

Teacher Tips

☀ Move through the book as you see fit. The writing activities are given in alphabetical order, but feel free to jump around. Do them in any order you choose.

☀ You may find that some activities are too advanced for your students, while others may be too basic. Some activities may take more time than you have on a particular day. Others may take less time than you planned. Revise or extend tasks to suit your students' needs.

☀ Use the writing tasks in this book as full lessons, warm-ups, homework assignments, writing center activities, group projects, or performance assessments.

☀ Recycle any specific forms, charts, or graphic organizers to fit other writing activities you may pursue with your students.

☀ Determine the best grouping to suit your teaching style, and students' learning styles and independence levels. Invite them to work individually, in pairs, in small groups, or as a whole class.

☀ For whole-class activities, copy the graphic organizers onto chart paper or onto transparencies for enlarged versions.

☀ Encourage students to discuss, share, question, analyze, and summarize each other's writing. Foster an atmosphere that promotes exploration, appreciation, and respect for one another as writers, thinkers, and problem-solvers. Help them feel confident and comfortable enough to choose to write on their own, without external prompts or assignments.

◉ Set up a writing center in your classroom. You can place some of these activities for students to do on their own in the center, and you can present examples of completed works and works-in-progress. Provide a variety of writing supplies, story starters, visual cues, word lists, dictionaries, thesauruses, inspiring quotations, author biographies, and so on.

◉ Take advantage of writing opportunities that present themselves on any given day. Talk about these opportunities, work out a pre-writing plan, develop criteria, or model a finished product—whichever suits the task.

◉ Be a role model. Show that you, too, are a working writer who must think about, plan, try out, fix, and polish your own work until you are satisfied with it.

◉ Involve parents. Present some of these writing ideas at parent meetings or conferences to highlight the value of this component in your language arts program.

A Is for Alphabet

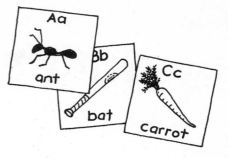

Objective: Students contribute to a collaborative alphabet book.

Get Ready . . .

❂ Engage students by singing the alphabet song, as well as other songs, such as "Alligators All Around" from *Really Rosie.*

❂ Share a variety of favorite alphabet books, such as *Alphabatics* by Suse MacDonald, *Butterfly Alphabet* by Kjell B. Sandved, or *ABC Discovery!* by Izhar Cohen. Compare and contrast the formats these books use. Pose questions such as the following: "Are there words given for each letter?" "Do the words stand alone?" "Are they part of a sentence? A riddle? A poem?" "How do starting letters stand out?" "Do all the words go together in some way, such as kinds of animals, flowers, or actions?" "What makes you like one book more than another?"

❂ Play an informal game in which students draw a letter of the alphabet from a box and then the entire class brainstorms to name words that begin with that letter.

Get Set . . .

❂ Tell students that they are going to work on pages for a class ABC book. Duplicate and distribute the form on page 10. Be sure students understand how to use the page.

❂ Divide the class into pairs or small groups. Assign each group one or more letters of the alphabet. The groups will create pages for those letters for the collaborative alphabet book.

❂ Provide dictionaries so students can browse for ideas and confirm spelling.

❂ You may want to determine an overriding theme for groups to use, such as animals, places, foods, city life, the country, the seashore, tools and machines, and so on.

Write!

❂ Encourage students to brainstorm for the best possible words for their letters.

❂ Remind students to illustrate their word choices.

Get Together

❂ As a class, organize the book. Have students say the alphabet aloud to signal each writer to present his or her completed page(s) in alphabetical order. Ask the class to work together to design a cover for the book.

❂ Challenge students to add words to the pages before you bind the book. Keep a running list of words to add to future publications.

❂ Extend by having students share the collaborative book with younger children. Ask the librarian to feature the book in the school library; invite comments and reviews from other readers.

Quick & Fun Writing Activities Just for Young Learners • Scholastic Professional Books

Name _____

A Is for Alphabet

is for _____

is also for _____

_____

_____

_____

10

B Is for Book Review

Objective: Students explore two ways to interest readers in a book.

Get Ready . . .

◉ Engage students by reading aloud. Choose material likely to engender strong responses. Discuss questions such as the following: "What did you like best about this book?" "Which character was your favorite, and why?" "What problem got solved in the story?" "How was the problem solved?" "What surprised you?"

◉ Talk about the purpose of a book review. Explain that it is a short piece of writing that tells about a book and gets others interested in reading it.

◉ Explain that another way to interest people in a book is to create an inviting cover, or *jacket*, for it. Display some appealing jackets for books that students know. Point out common elements, such as an illustration of some character or part of the story. Highlight any *blurbs*, or brief comments about the book, that appear.

◉ Tell students that another way to interest new readers in a book is to list some key things that happen in it. This approach also helps the reviewer focus on the book's main ideas. Read aloud the inside flap copy of a book cover.

◉ Guide students in selecting suitable books to review. They may work alone or in pairs.

Get Set . . .

◉ Tell students that they are going to design a book jacket and plan a book review. Duplicate and distribute the Book Jacket Form (page 12) and the Problem/Solution Chart (page 13). Be sure students understand how to use the pages. They may complete the pages in either order.

◉ If you typically use a standard book review form, display it. Encourage students to look for similarities and differences between it and the form used in this activity.

Write!

◉ To help them formulate and state ideas succinctly, suggest that students talk to each other as they write.

◉ Allow students to refer to the book they are reviewing for the correct spelling of the title, the author and/or illustrator, character names, and other important details.

◉ Remind students not to replicate the book's existing jacket. Have them create their own version that will attract new readers.

Get Together

◉ Have students display their book jackets as they present details of the Problem/Solution Chart to classmates. Make sure that students don't "spill the beans" to future readers.

◉ Extend the activity by having students write letters to authors or illustrators.

Name _____

B Is for Book Review

Make a new cover for a book.

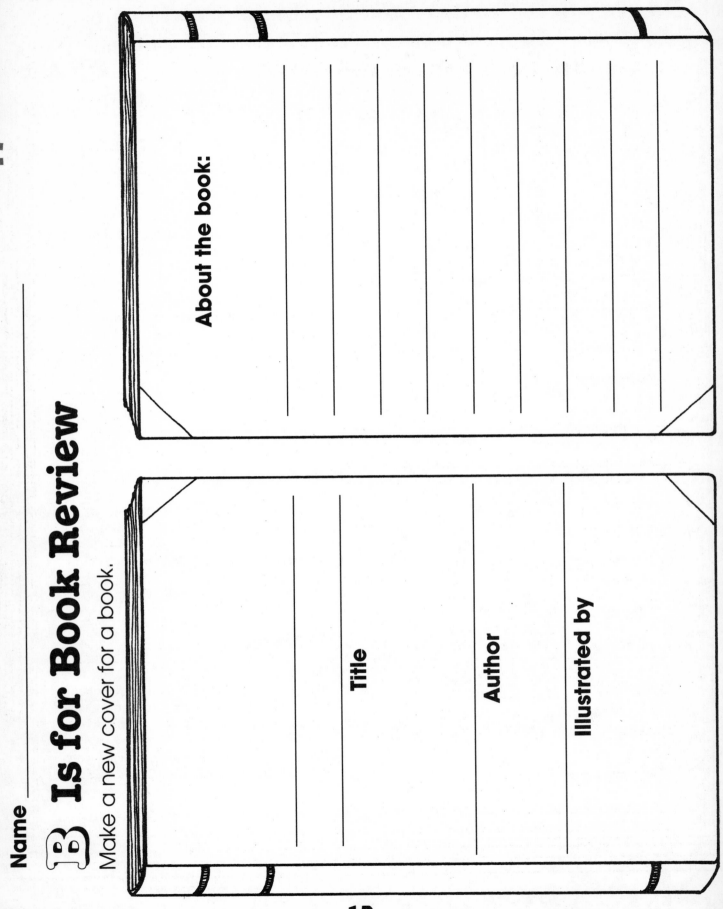

About the book:

Title

Author

Illustrated by

Name _____

B Is for Book Review

Complete the chart for your book.

Title _____

Author _____

Illustrator _____

Main Character(s) _____

_____

Problem(s) _____

_____

_____

_____

Solution(s) _____

_____

_____

_____

Surprise(s) _____

_____

_____

C Is for Compare and Contrast

Objective: Students complete a graphic organizer to compare and contrast characters.

◼◼ Get Ready . . .

❀ Engage students by displaying two seemingly disparate objects, such as a math book and a milk carton. Ask them to tell how the objects are obviously different. Then challenge them to think of ways in which the items are alike (i.e., both made of paper; both have corners; both have words on them). Encourage creative thinking!

❀ Write the words *compare* and *contrast* on the board. Clarify their meanings as follows:

> We **compare** when we say how things are *alike*.
>
> We **contrast** when we say how things are *different*.

❀ Display pairs of pictures of animals, famous people, or fictional characters. Ask students to compare and contrast the pictures in each pair.

◼◼ Get Set . . .

❀ Tell students that they are going to use a chart to compare and contrast characters. Duplicate and distribute the Compare and Contrast Chart on page 15. Be sure students understand how to use the page.

❀ Guide students in selecting two characters to compare and contrast. They may focus on two characters from the same work or from different works, a fictional and a non-fictional character, figures from the past or present, or one from each category. Alternatively, you may prefer to specify the two characters you would like students to examine.

◼◼ Write!

❀ Before students complete the chart, have them brainstorm or free-write to list features or traits unique to each character. Explain that features or traits that both characters share belong in the center of the chart.

❀ Present this task as a small-group activity to accompany a book talk. Group members can take turns adding their ideas to the chart.

❀ Pair emergent writers with more advanced writers.

◼◼ Get Together

❀ Post the Compare and Contrast Charts on a bulletin board or compile them in a binder.

❀ Challenge students to complete another Compare and Contrast Chart about characters, ideas, or situations that appear in other curriculum areas. Relate this graphic organizer to the Venn diagrams they might encounter in math lessons.

❀ Extend by having students design alternate versions of Compare and Contrast Charts.

Quick & Fun Writing Activities Just for Young Learners • Scholastic Professional Books

Name

Is Compare and Contrast

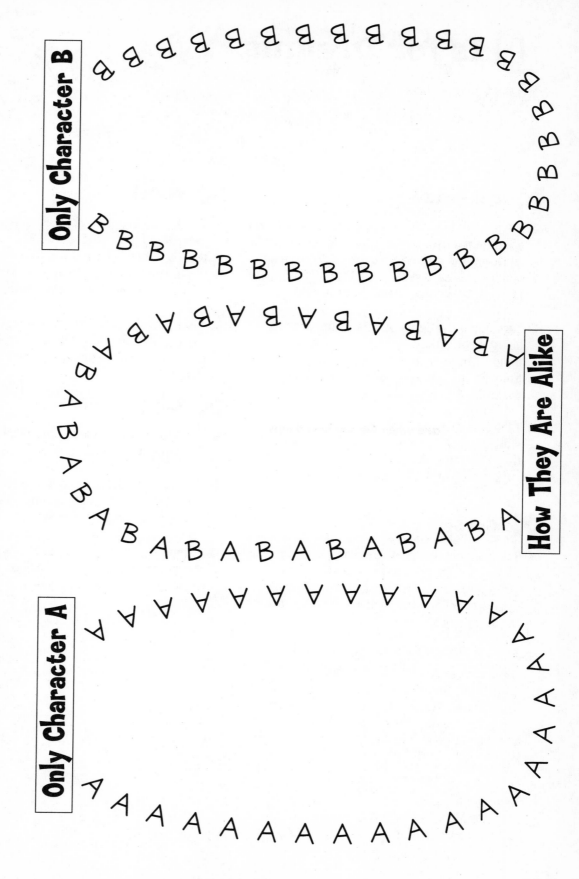

Only Character B

How They Are Alike

Only Character A

15

D Is for Dreams

Objective: *Students record snippets of daydreams or nighttime dreams and elaborate upon one.*

Get Ready . . .

◉ Engage students by recalling stories in which a main character has an amazing dream, such as Dorothy did in *The Wizard of Oz*, or read aloud *Ben's Dream* by Chris Van Allsburg or *Cowboy Dreams* by Dayal Kaur Khalsa.

◉ Turn down the lights. Ask students to think about dreams they've had that stick in their minds. These memorable dreams might be funny, scary, puzzling, silly, weird, sad, or wishful.

◉ Talk about ways to sort the kinds of dreams students have experienced. For instance, they can think about nighttime dreams, daydreams, and nightmares (bad dreams).

Get Set . . .

◉ Tell students that they are going to describe a dream. Duplicate and distribute the Dream Diagram Form on page 17 and the Dream Description Form on page 18. Be sure students understand how to use these pages.

◉ Have students brainstorm on their own or daydream to recollect dream memories. When they finish, invite pairs or small groups to share ideas. From this discussion, each student can decide which of his or her dreams to describe in greater detail.

Write!

◉ The Dream Diagram Form is meant as a free-association tool. Students should complete this page first. Then, when they have chosen the dream they wish to describe in detail, they should use the Dream Description Form.

◉ Allow emergent writers to tell their dream story to a scribe who can help write it down, or they can speak into a tape recorder.

Get Together

◉ Invite students to share their Dream Descriptions in small groups.

◉ Challenge students to act out dreams for classmates, or to make up endings for dreams that ended abruptly.

◉ Extend by having students free-write to evocative music, and then elaborate upon some of these daydream ideas.

Quick & Fun Writing Activities Just for Young Learners • Scholastic Professional Books

Name _____

D Is for Dreams

Quick & Fun Writing Activities Just for Young Learners • Scholastic Professional Books

Name _____

D Is for Dreams

Wow, what a dream I had! This is what I remember:

_____

_____

_____

_____

_____

_____

_____

_____

_____

_____

_____

_____

_____

_____

And then I woke up!

Quick & Fun Writing Activities Just for Young Learners • Scholastic Professional Books

E Is for Expert

Objective: Students focus on particular areas of expertise and how they became experts.

Get Ready . . .

- ❂ Ask students what it means to be an expert. Help them understand that an expert is someone who is very skilled at something, or who knows a lot about a certain subject. Introduce the word *expertise*, and explain its meaning (expert knowledge or experience).

- ❂ Talk about how people get to be experts. Some people become experts at things they are very interested in or do a lot, such as dinosaurs or sports. Other people study or take lessons to become experts, such as in medicine or in music. Help students recognize that everyone is an expert on something.

- ❂ Engage students by asking groups to consider ways to complete statements like the following:

  > If I needed expert advice on pets, I might ask _____ .

  > If I needed expert advice on the weather, I might ask _____ .

  > If I needed expert advice on sports, I might ask _____ .

- ❂ Ask leading questions to help students determine their own areas of expertise: "What are your hobbies?" "What things do you know about that most other kids don't know?" "What are you really good at?" "What do you like to learn about?"

Get Set . . .

- ❂ Tell students that they are going to write about their expertise and then give expert tips to

others. Duplicate and distribute the Expert Form on page 20. Have students complete this page first and then use it to help them with the Expert Tips Form on page 21. Be sure students understand how to use these pages.

Write!

- ❂ Invite students to share ideas as they write. Emergent writers can dictate their ideas to an aide or into a tape recorder.

- ❂ Explain that a "gem of wisdom" means an important piece of information that is very useful. Tell students that, as experts, they can offer a few "gems" that may be helpful or enlightening to others.

Get Together

- ❂ Have students describe their expertise in small groups or in front of the class.

- ❂ Challenge students to suggest activities or projects that fit their particular areas of expertise. Some of these ideas might become viable small-group or class projects.

- ❂ Extend by having students give oral presentations to support their expertise. For instance, a student might play the flute for the class; another might demonstrate how to make an origami crane; another might do impressions of TV characters.

19

Name _____

E Is for Expert

Everyone is an expert on something.
Write about a way in which you are an expert.

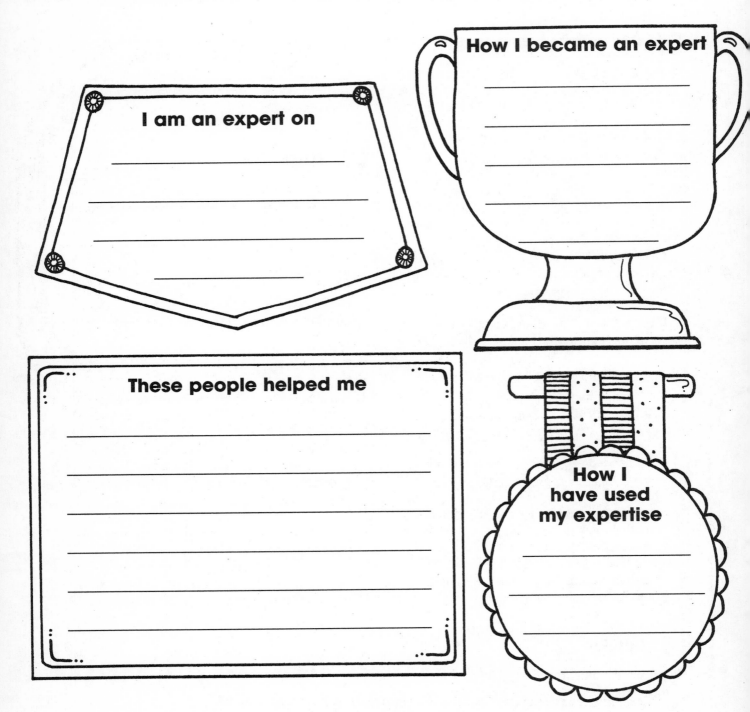

I am an expert on
_____
_____
_____
_____

How I became an expert
_____
_____
_____
_____
_____

These people helped me
_____
_____
_____
_____
_____
_____

How I
have used
my expertise
_____
_____
_____

20

Name _____

E Is for Expert

I am an expert on _____.
I want to share some tips about what I know.
Here are my "gems of wisdom."

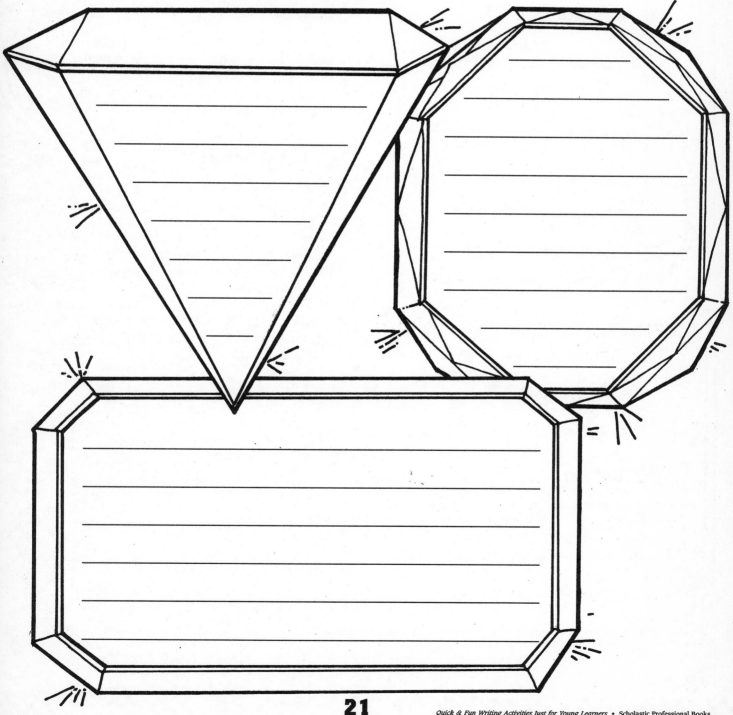

Quick & Fun Writing Activities Just for Young Learners • Scholastic Professional Books

F Is for Feelings

Objective: Students respond to visual prompts to describe different kinds of feelings. Then they write about times when they experienced the feelings.

Get Ready . . .

❂ Engage students by sharing the books *Feelings* by Aliki, and/or *I Feel Orange Today* by Patricia Godwin.

❂ Sing songs about feelings, such as "Who's Afraid of the Big Bad Wolf?" or "If You're Happy and You Know It, Clap Your Hands."

❂ Display pictures of facial expressions to suggest a range of feelings, such as happiness, sadness, anger, frustration, surprise, confusion, courage, and so on. Ask students to identify the feelings and to mimic the faces.

❂ Play an informal game in which a student makes a face and classmates guess what feeling he or she is showing. Model this idea for the class, and then have students play in small groups.

❂ If you have access to a camera, take candid photos of student's faces, making an effort to capture a wide range of expressions. Display the pictures on a class bulletin board.

Get Set . . .

❂ Tell students that they are going to explore feelings. Duplicate and distribute the Feelings Faces on pages 23-24. Be sure students understand how to use the pages.

Write!

❂ Invite students to talk to each other as they write. This will help them formulate ideas.

❂ Allow emergent writers to dictate their ideas to an aide or into a tape recorder.

Get Together

❂ Have students share their feelings faces in small groups.

❂ Challenge students to associate different feelings with particular colors, animals, or places. For instance, red might suggest anger; a deer might suggest fear.

❂ Extend by having students draw their own feelings faces and write about times when they felt that way.

Name _____

 Is for Feelings

Look at each face.
What feelings do you see?
List some feeling words that fit.

_____

_____

_____

_____

_____

_____

_____

_____

23

Name _____

F Is for Feelings

Circle one of the faces.

Write about a time when you felt this way.

_____

_____

_____

_____

_____

_____

_____

_____

_____

_____

_____

24

G Is for Greetings

Objective: Students plan and create original greeting cards for different occasions.

Get Ready . . .

- Engage students by displaying an assortment of greeting cards designed for birthdays, holidays, and anniversaries. Also include congratulations cards, as well as get well, thank you, and friendship cards. Show regular cards, pop-up cards, accordion-fold cards, window cards, and cut-out cards to show the wide variety of options.

- Discuss questions like the following: "Why do people send greeting cards?" "Have you ever bought a greeting card for someone?" "What do you look for in a card?" "Have you ever made a card for someone?" "Do you like funny cards, serious cards, mushy cards, or plain cards?" "Which kind of card do you like to receive?"

- Brainstorm a list of occasions or reasons to send greeting cards. In addition to those already mentioned, don't forget cards that offer personal wishes, such as *Get well, I'm sorry, Thank you, I miss you, Good luck,* or *Congratulations.*

Get Set . . .

- Tell students that they are going to plan and make greeting cards. Duplicate and distribute the Greeting Card Planners on pages 26-27. Be sure students understand how to use these pages.

- Provide art supplies, such as construction paper, scissors, markers, tape, stickers, glitter, and anything else that students can use to make and decorate their cards.

Write!

- People spend money on fancy store-bought greeting cards, but nothing beats a card with a personal touch. Encourage students to put a little of themselves in their messages. Suggest ways they can customize their cards to fit the recipients: Use the person's favorite colors, draw pictures of things the person likes, use words or expressions the person says, and so on.

- Invite students to add special touches to their cards, such as lace, pinked edges, ribbons, feathers, fabric scraps, foil, perfume, or pictures cut from magazines.

Get Together

- Have students share, display, and/or send their cards.

- Challenge students to create original greeting cards for silly and/or made-up occasions, such as National Tooth Fairy Day, Smile Day, or Be-Kind-To-Your-Pet Day, and so on.

- Extend by having students make "just-thinking-of-you" cards for school employees who are often overlooked, such as janitors, cooks, bus drivers, or office workers.

25

Name _____

G Is for Greetings

Here are some kinds of cards you can make.

Regular Card

Stand-Up Card

Pop-up Card

Accordion Card

Window Card

Which kind of card do you like best?

_____

_____

Name _____

G Is for Greetings

Make a greeting card for someone.
The table below shows some words and phrases to use.

Reason for Card	Ending Words	Other Words to Use
Happy Birthday Happy Anniversary Your Special Day Holiday Get Well Soon THANK YOU Congratulations Friendship I Miss You I'm Sorry	Best Wishes! Congratulations! Love, Sincerely, Always, From the bottom of my heart, Hugs and kisses, All the best, Many happy returns,	Greetings Celebrate Merry Favorite Surprise Grateful Joy Amazing SPECIAL Remember

Greeting card checklist:

☐ Who is the card for? _____

☐ What is the reason for the card? _____

☐ What kind of card will you make? _____

☐ Design and make your card.

☐ Write a message inside your card.

☐ Sign your card.

☐ Give or send your card.

H Is for Hero

Objective: Students generate brief sketches of people they consider to be heroes.

Get Ready . . .

⚙ Engage students by reading selections from *The Children's Book of Heroes* by William J. Bennett.

⚙ Generate a list of qualities that heroes posses. Help students distinguish between people who are merely famous, such as athletes or movie stars, and those who have done something truly heroic. You might brainstorm a list of words associated with heroes, such as *brave, generous, helpful, bold, daring, fearless, strong, independent,* or *selfless.*

⚙ Have students tell stories they know about heroes, real or fictional, past or present.

⚙ Create an interactive "Wall of Heroes." Display names and pictures of well-known heroes, such as Martin Luther King, Anne Frank, or Abraham Lincoln. Include local heroes who have helped your community. Add to the wall all year.

Get Set . . .

⚙ Tell students that they are going to write about a hero. Remind them to draw a picture or paste a photograph of their hero on the Hero Form on page 29.

⚙ Duplicate and distribute the Hero Form. Be sure students understand how to use the page.

Write!

⚙ Invite students to talk to each other as they write. This will help them shape their thinking. Peer editors can help each other focus on the essence of heroism.

⚙ Hold informal conversations with students about their chosen heroes. Ask leading questions that can help them pinpoint the qualities that make their heroes stand out.

⚙ Allow emergent writers to dictate their ideas to an aide or into a tape recorder.

Get Together

⚙ Have students share their hero sketches in small groups or with the class.

⚙ Challenge students to find different ways to group the heroes. For instance, they might sort them by heroes of the past versus heroes of the present. They might group political or military heroes separately from social or personal heroes.

⚙ Extend by having students tell or write about something heroic they have done to help someone else or that someone has done for them.

Quick & Fun Writing Activities Just for Young Learners • Scholastic Professional Books

Name _____

H Is for Hero

Who is your hero? Fill out the form below.

MY HERO

_____
(name)

This person is my hero because _____
_____.

My hero is especially great because _____
_____.

To honor my hero, I would like to _____
_____.

If I gave an award to my hero, I would call it _____
_____.

If I could say one thing to my hero, I would say, _____
_____.

I Is for Interview

Objective: Students prepare to conduct interviews to gather information.

Get Ready . . .

- Define an *interview* as a face-to-face meeting in which someone asks questions to gather information. Remind students that they have probably seen interviews on television talk shows, celebrity features, or news reports.

- Share parts of interviews that have appeared in children's magazines.

- Clarify the difference between a *conversation* and an *interview*. Both are forms of talking. Point out that the main goals of an interview are to gather facts and details from someone and to record the information to use later. A good interviewer plans a set of questions in advance to keep the conversation moving in the right direction.

Get Set . . .

- Tell students that they are going to plan and conduct an interview. Duplicate and distribute the Interview Forms on pages 31-32. (You may need to duplicate more than one copy of the Interview Form on page 32 for each student.) Be sure students understand how to use these pages.

- Talk about the "10 Good Ideas for Good Interviews" on page 31. Remind students that the interviewee is doing them a favor. This means that it is especially important to be polite and fair, and to be prepared so they won't take up too much of the person's time.

Write!

- Help students determine whom to interview and what information to gather from that person. Guide them to summarize their goal in a main-idea statement.

- It may help students begin by listing all the questions they can think of, regardless of order. Then they can go back and edit their list to include only the most pertinent questions, in the most sensible order.

- Invite pairs of students to role-play an interview so they can get a sense of what it is like to direct the questions and jot down the responses.

- Allow time for students to conduct their interviews in school or outside of school.

Get Together

- Invite students to share their interview experiences. You might challenge them to do a self-evaluation that may help them in future interview situations. You might also suggest that they use their notes to write a brief report summarizing the interview and then share it with the class.

- Extend by having small groups of students plan and conduct team interviews. Use this technique for cross-curricular projects in science, social studies, music, or health.

Quick & Fun Writing Activities Just for Young Learners • Scholastic Professional Books

Name _____

I Is for Interview

The point of an interview is to gather information.
Anybody can conduct an interview. Here's how it works:

You are the interviewer.

The interviewer *asks* the questions.

The person you interview is the interviewee.

The interviewee *answers* the questions.

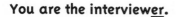

10 Good Ideas for Good Interviews

1. Prepare your questions ahead of time. Practice with a friend. Get your questions in order.

2. Introduce yourself. Shake hands. Get comfortable before you begin.

3. Tell the main goal of your interview. This helps the interviewee to give better answers.

4. Always be polite and friendly! Remember to say *please* and *thank you.*

5. Ask questions clearly. Listen carefully to the answers! Keep your mind on the interview at all times.

6. Jot down key details so you will remember them later. Use a pad and pencil or a tape recorder.

7. Ask the interviewee to explain anything you don't understand. It's okay to add a question to help you understand something.

8. Keep your interview to 10-15 minutes. Before you end, make sure you have the facts and details you need.

9. Thank the interviewee. Say good-bye and shake hands.

10. Write a thank-you note to the interviewee. Include a copy of what you wrote based on the interview.

Name _____

I Is for Interview

Write your questions on this form.
Write the interviewee's answers below the questions.
You may also use another sheet of paper.

Interviewee: _____

Main Goal of the Interview: _____
_____

Question 1 _____
_____?

Answer: _____
_____.

Question 2 _____
_____?

Answer: _____
_____.

Question 3 _____
_____?

Answer: _____
_____.

J Is for Joke Journal

Hee Hee!

Objective: Students collect jokes and riddles to contribute to collaborative joke projects.

Get Ready . . .

- Engage students by sharing jokes from such books as *1000 Crazy Jokes for Kids* by Michael Johnstone, *The Little Giant Book of Knock-Knocks* by Charles Keller, or *1,000 More Jokes for Kids* by Michael Kilgarriff.

- Sing folksongs based on jokes or riddles, such as "What Did Della Ware?" or "I Gave My Love a Cherry."

- Discuss joke vocabulary. For instance, clarify the difference between a *joke* (a short story with an ending meant to make people laugh) and a *riddle* (a tricky, funny, or puzzling question). Explain the meaning of *punch line* (the funny part at the end), *set-up* (the beginning of a joke that sets the scene or introduces the characters), and *pun* (a joke based on the double meaning of words that sound alike).

- Give examples of different kinds of jokes, such as the "Knock-Knock joke," the "elephant joke," the "groaner," or the "Tom Swifty" (based on puns).

Get Set . . .

- Tell students that they are going to write a favorite joke or riddle to contribute to a class collection. Duplicate and distribute the Joke Journal on page 34. Be sure students understand how to use the page. Provide as many copies as students need.

- Have partners interview each other about what makes a joke or riddle funny to them, why they like a certain joke or riddle, where they typically hear them, and what makes a good joke teller. The information that emerges can help guide students as they write.

Write!

- Have students try out their jokes or riddles on classmates. Students can tell the jokes or riddles first, for practice, and then write them down. Finally, they can read what they have written to make sure it is complete and correct.

- Students who write riddles might want to use different colors for the questions and answers. They also might want to highlight the punch line of a joke with a colored marker.

Get Together

- Have students share their jokes in small groups, with the class, or record them on video.

- Hold a Joke-A-Thon, in which students present jokes in round-robin fashion.

- Make sound effects, such as groans, honking horns, penny whistle sounds, drum shots, and so forth, to indicate the end of a joke or riddle. Record these in advance, if possible.

- Extend by helping students compile a class joke book, a class joke tape, or a joke-of-the-day calendar. You might consider ways to use these products as the basis for a fundraiser or community outreach project.

Quick & Fun Writing Activities Just for Young Learners • Scholastic Professional Books

Name _____

J Is for Joke Journal

Say, have you heard this one???

Write your joke or riddle below.

_____

_____

_____

_____

_____

_____

_____

Why it's funny:

_____

_____

_____

Where did you hear your joke or riddle?

_____

_____

_____

K Is for Kite

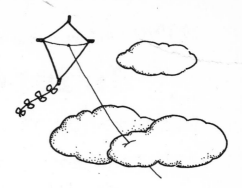

Objective: *Students write an observation piece from the perspective of a kite high up in the sky.*

Get Ready . . .

- Engage students by sharing excerpts from books about kites, such as *Catch the Wind! All About Kites* by Gail Gibbons, *One Windy Day* by Jane Caraway, or *The Great Kite Book* by Norman Schmidt. You might also read the poem "The Kite" by Harry Behn.

- Have students memorize and then recite together the following anonymous poem about kites:

    "Sometimes I sit and wish that I
    Could be a kite up in the sky,
    And float upon the breeze and go
    Whichever way I chance to blow."

- Discuss the expression *bird's-eye view.* Tell students that it describes the view from high above, as a bird might see it. Invite students to share experiences they have had with bird's-eye views, such as from airplanes, Ferris wheels, observation towers, rooftops, and so on.

Get Set . . .

- Tell students that they are going to write what they might see from up high—a "kite's-eye view." Duplicate and distribute the Kite Form on page 36. Be sure students understand how to use the page. Notice that it includes the poem they have learned.

Write!

- Invite students to close their eyes and use their imaginations before they write. Point out that they can use the ribbons on the kite's tail for words or ideas to remember.

- To create a free feeling, play soft, airy music as students write. You might try some Native American or Japanese flute music, Andean pipe tunes, or recorded birdcalls.

Get Together

- Have students share their "lofty" observations. One way is to suspend the Kite Forms from a clothesline strung across the room.

- Extend by having students make and launch message kites. These are simple paper kites (or balloons) that include the student's name, school name and address, date, and a brief message to the potential finder. The message asks for a return letter or postcard describing how and where the kite was found.

- Plan a field trip to a high spot, such as an observation deck, a skyscraper, a fire tower, or a penthouse. Encourage students to look down and write about what they see and how it makes them feel.

Quick & Fun Writing Activities Just for Young Learners • Scholastic Professional Books

Name _____

K Is for Kite

Read the poem below.

> **Sometimes I sit and wish that I**
> **Could be a kite up in the sky,**
> **And float upon the breeze and go**
> **Whichever way I chance to blow.**

Pretend that you are a kite in the sky.
You look down. What do you see?
Write about what you see.

L Is for Letter

Objective: Students fill in a template to write business letters and to address envelopes.

Get Ready . . .

◉ Build background about letters and the mail. If possible, take a field trip to a local post office, or invite a postal worker to address the class.

◉ Tell students that a business letter is a special kind of letter written to someone the writer may not know. It is different from a friendly letter because it is formal and polite, and usually asks for or gives information, or offers an opinion.

◉ Talk about the parts of a business letter: the return address, date, inside address, greeting, message, closing, and signature. Discuss why each part is important.

◉ Brainstorm a list of people that students might write to, such as a famous person, a favorite author, the president, a fictional character, a hero, a toy company, the head of a TV station, an astronaut, and so on. You might generate a list that students can refer to.

◉ Demonstrate how to fold a business letter into thirds so that it fits in a standard #10 envelope. Give students time to practice this skill.

Get Set . . .

◉ Tell students that they are going to write a letter and address an envelope. Duplicate and distribute the Letter and Envelope Templates on pages 38-39. Be sure students know how to use the pages.

Write!

◉ Help students decide to whom they wish to write. Peer partners can talk over ideas.

◉ Guide students in filling in the standard parts of the Letter Template first. Then have them focus on the message they wish to convey in the body of the letter.

Get Together

◉ Have students actually mail their letters. You may need to help them determine the correct addresses. Hopefully, they will get some responses.

◉ Challenge students to exchange letters and pretend to be the recipient. They can then reply, answering as they imagine that the person or character might.

◉ Keep a supply of blank Letter Templates available for any class letter-writing needs.

Quick & Fun Writing Activities Just for Young Learners • Scholastic Professional Books

Name _____

L Is for Letter

Use this form. It shows all parts of a business letter.

Write your address here. ➡ _____
Give the street, city, state, _____
and ZIP code. _____

Write today's ➡ _____
date here.

_____ ⬅ **Write the business**
address here.

_____

_____ **Write the greeting here.**
Then write the message.

Dear _____ :

_____

_____

_____

_____

_____

_____

_____

Write the closing here. ➡ _____

Write your name here. ➡ _____

Name _____

L Is for Letter

Write the address on the envelope.
Remember to write clearly and neatly.

Write the return address here.
This is *your* address.

A stamp goes here.

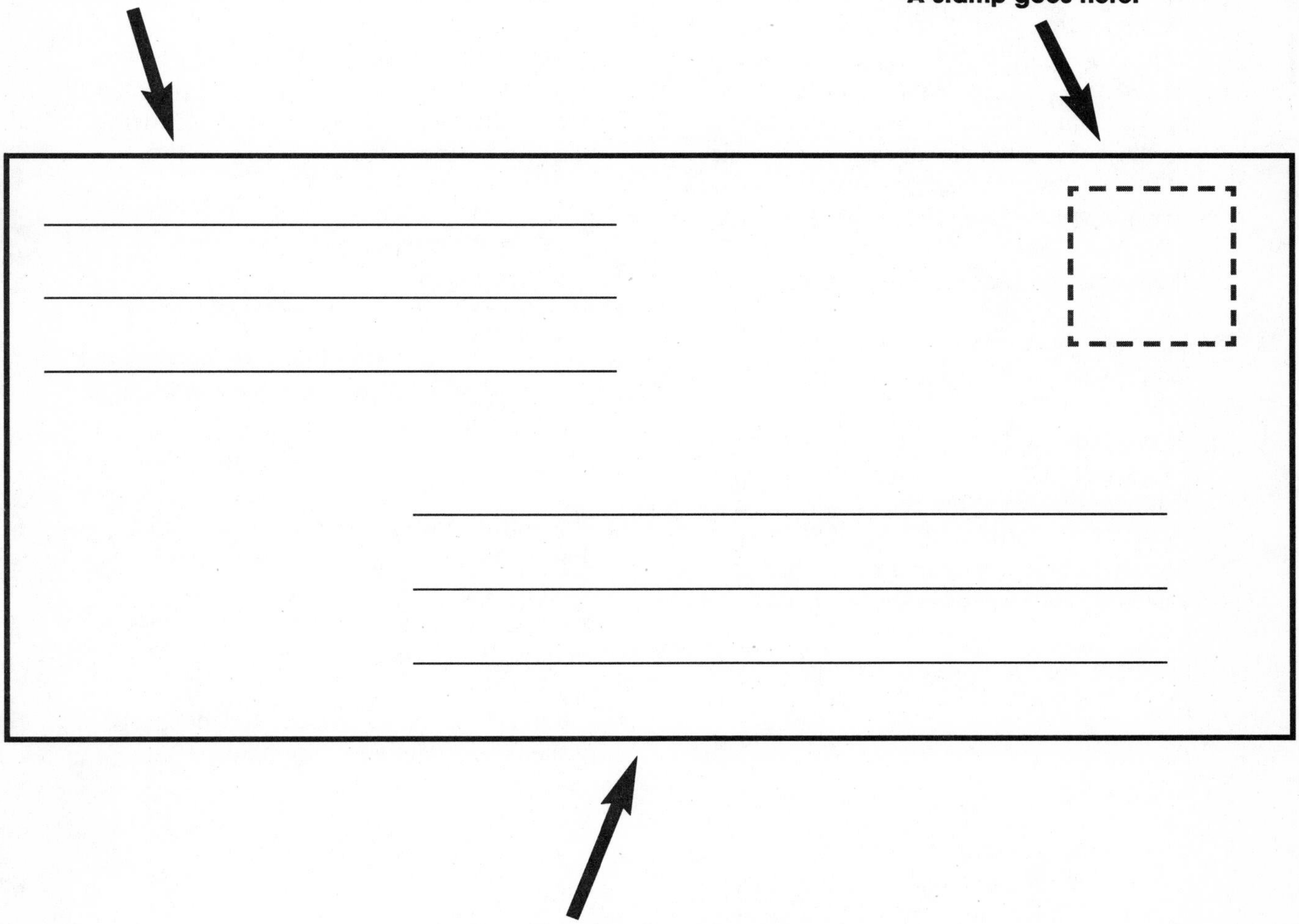

_____

_____

_____

_____

_____

_____

Write the mailing address here.
It's the name and address of the person you are writing.

Quick & Fun Writing Activities Just for Young Learners • Scholastic Professional Books

M Is for Magic Lantern

Objective: Students describe three wishes they would like to make.

Get Ready

- Engage students by sharing fairy tales about magic lanterns and wishes, such as *Aladdin and the Wonderful Lamp* by David Eastman, *The Fish Who Could Wish* by John Bush, *I Had a Lot of Wishes* by James Stevenson, or *The Three Wishes* by Margot Zemach. Talk about similarities and differences in stories like these. For example, in most such stories, the main characters usually don't foresee how a wish might backfire. People are sometimes apt to make greedy wishes, or the character who grants the wish may be a trickster.

- Sing wish songs, such as "When You Wish Upon a Star" or "If I Had a Hammer."

- Discuss familiar customs that involve making wishes. For instance, someone may make a wish before blowing out the candles on a birthday cake. Others wish on the first star they see or before they break a wishbone. Brainstorm for a list of wishing events.

- Talk about the old saying, "Be careful what you wish for; it might come true!"

Get Set . . .

- Tell students that they are going to write three wishes. Duplicate and distribute the Magic Lantern Wish List on page 41. Be sure students understand how to use the page.

Write!

- Turn out the lights for a few moments. Have students think quietly about the kinds of wishes that they would like to make.

- If students are having difficulty, suggest that they make three different kinds of wishes: one for themselves, one for family or friends, and one for the world.

Get Together

- Have students share their favorite wishes with partners.

- Challenge students to think of how an apparently simple wish could go awry if it were granted by an impish genie or a trickster.

- Extend by cutting apart the wishes and putting them into a bag or box. Each day, invite a students to pick a wish from the box and read it aloud. Students might enjoy guessing who originally made the wish.

- Set up a "Wish Wall" where students post wishes they write on sticky notes.

Quick & Fun Writing Activities Just for Young Learners • Scholastic Professional Books

Name _____

M Is for Magic Lantern

What if you had three wishes?
Think very carefully. Then write your wishes below.

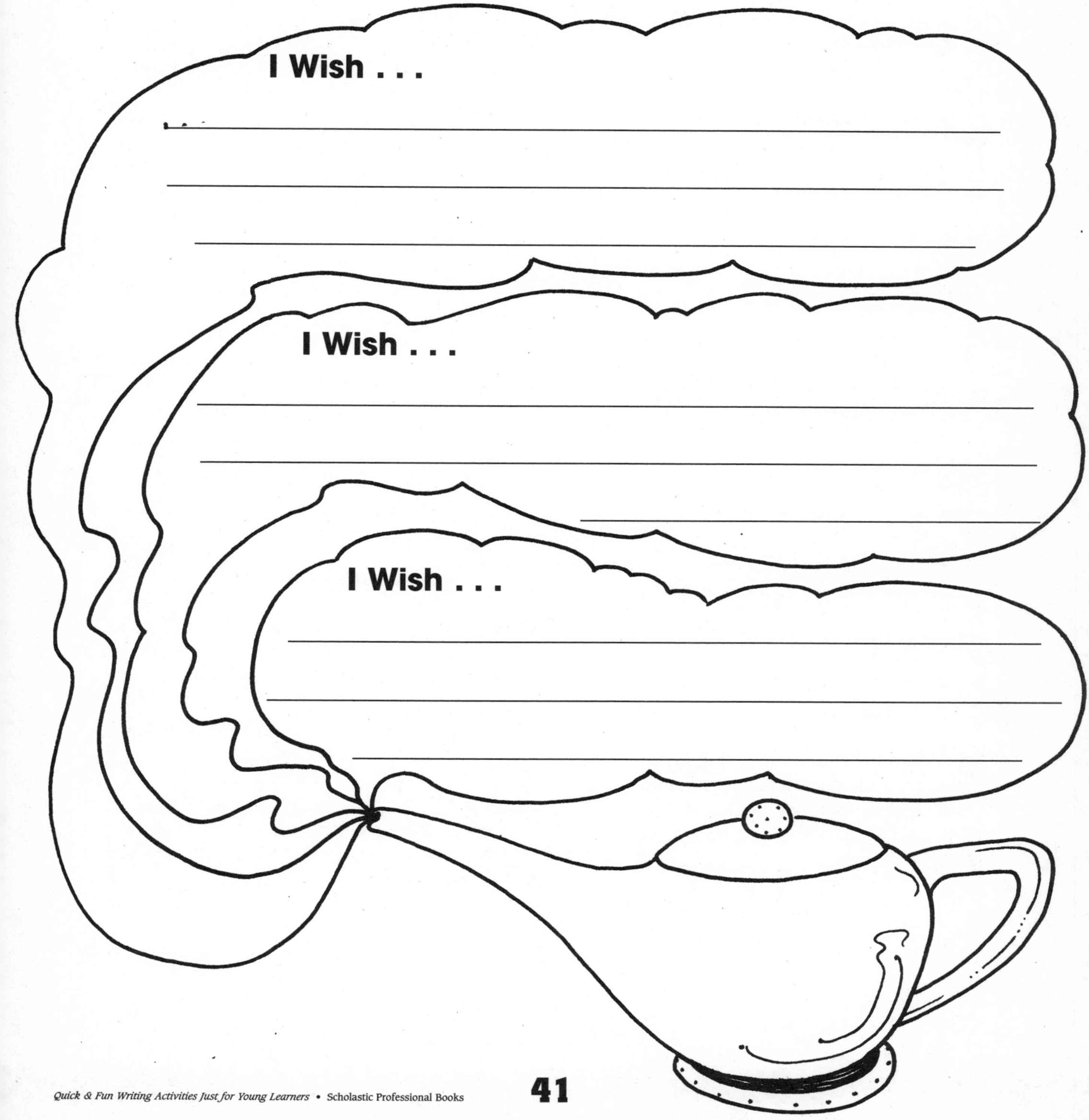

I Wish . . .

_____

_____

_____

I Wish . . .

_____

_____

_____

I Wish . . .

_____

_____

_____

41

N Is for Name

Objective: Students write descriptions in the form of acrostics based on the letters in their names.

Get Ready . . .

✹ Engage students by writing the letters of your name in a vertical column on the board. Challenge them to think of a *word* to describe you that begins with each letter. Jot down their ideas. Example:

> **M**other
> **E**ager
> **G**enerous

✹ Now, using the initial letters of another name, have students suggest a *short descriptive phrase* for each letter. Again, the goal is to create a sketch of a person. Example:

> **J**okes with friends after school,
> **O**wns an old purple truck,
> **N**ever has a mean thing to say!

✹ Explain that this kind of writing is called an *acrostic.* An acrostic is an arrangement of lines whose first letters spell out a word or phrase when read from top to bottom.

Get Set . . .

✹ Tell students that they are going to write an acrostic based on the letters in a name. Duplicate and distribute the Name Acrostic Form on page 43. Be sure students understand how to use it.

✹ Invite students to make an acrostic based on their own name, or on the name of a friend, family member, or classmate. Help them choose whether to use their first name, nickname, middle name, last name, or any or all of them!

Write!

✹ Allow students to browse through a dictionary or word list for ideas.

✹ If a name has repeated letters, encourage students to come up with different words for each occurrence of the same letter.

✹ You might have small groups work on their name acrostics together so that they can benefit from a give-and-take of words and ideas.

Get Together

✹ Have students display their name acrostics on a bulletin board. Those with computer skills can publish their acrostics in bold style.

✹ Challenge students to create name acrostics for pets, places, or famous people.

✹ Extend by having students use the acrostic form for a science concept, a social studies project, or a study guide to remember facts or vocabulary words.

Quick & Fun Writing Activities Just for Young Learners • Scholastic Professional Books

Name _____

N Is for Name

Make an acrostic.

Write the letters of a name in the boxes.

Use as many boxes and lines as you need.

□ _____

□ _____

□ _____

□ _____

□ _____

□ _____

□ _____

□ _____

□ _____

□ _____

Quick & Fun Writing Activities Just for Young Learners • Scholastic Professional Books

O Is for Once Upon a Time . . .

Objective: *Students plan and write original fairy tales or retell old favorites.*

Get Ready . . .

☙ Engage students by reading aloud some fairy tales or folktales. *Misoso: Once Upon a Time Tales from Africa* by Verna Aardema is one useful source. Guide students in recognizing that a fairy tale is a make-believe story.

☙ Talk about the meaning of the words that often open and close many fairy tales: "Once upon a time . . ." and ". . . lived happily ever after."

☙ Discuss the key parts of a fairy tale: main characters; conflicts between good and evil, clever and mean, rich and poor, and so on; magical help; and, usually, a happy ending.

☙ Invite students to act out some well-known fairy tales with puppets or dolls.

Get Set . . .

☙ Tell students that they are going to plan and write fairy tales. Duplicate and distribute the Fairy Tale Planner, Title Page, and "Once Upon a Time . . ." Form on pages 45-47. Be sure students understand how to use these pages.

☙ Help students use the Fairy Tale Planner to jot down ideas for the fairy tale they will write. They use the Title Page to present the title of their fairy tale and a suitable illustration to support it. They use the "Once Upon a Time . . ." Form for a final draft.

Write!

☙ Invite students to talk to each other as they write, to set the scene, name characters, work out what happens, and so on. Hold informal conversations as they work to direct them as needed.

☙ Allow students who may have trouble writing original fairy tales to retell one they know. They will still benefit from the writing process as they recreate familiar tales.

Get Together

☙ Have students share their fairy tales aloud. You can also compile all the tales into a class fairy tale anthology. Bind it in a fanciful cover.

☙ Challenge students to compare and contrast their fairy tales with well-known ones.

☙ Extend by having students read their tales to younger visitors. Consider having a Fairy Tale Day in which students dress up as characters from favorite fairy tales, old or new.

44

Name _____

Ⓞ Is for Once Upon a Time . . .

Plan your fairy tale.

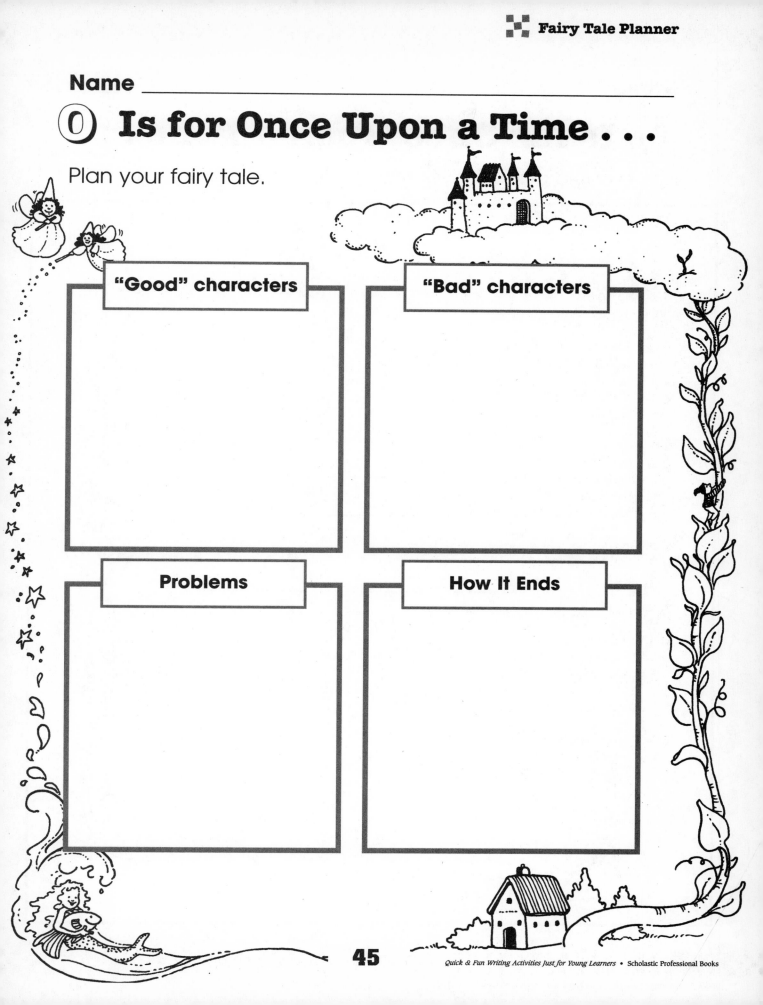

"Good" characters

"Bad" characters

Problems

How It Ends

Name _____

⓪ Is for Once Upon a Time . . .

Make a title page for your fairy tale.

_____

_____

_____

by _____

Quick & Fun Writing Activities Just for Young Learners • Scholastic Professional Books

Name _____

O Is for Once Upon a Time . . .

Write your final draft on this fairy tale paper.

Once upon a time _____

_____

_____

_____

_____

_____

_____

_____

_____

_____

_____

_____

_____

_____ lived happily ever after!

Quick & Fun Writing Activities Just for Young Learners • Scholastic Professional Books

P Is for Pet

Objective: *Students describe favorite pets—real or imagined.*

Get Ready . . .

❀ Engage students by reading aloud a pet book, such as *The Pet That I Want* by Mary Packard, *Pick a Pet* by Shelley Rotner, or *Can I Keep Him?* by Steven Kellogg.

❀ Create a "Pet Parade" display on a bulletin board or in a scrapbook. In it, post pictures students bring in of their own pets, or of pets they wish they could have.

❀ Discuss the duties involved in caring for a pet. Point out that responsible pet owners provide their pets with food, water, shelter, attention, and medical care, as needed.

Get Set . . .

❀ Tell students that they are going to write about pets they actually own or would like to have. Duplicate and distribute the Pet Idea Web, Pet Picture Page, and Pet Story Form on pages 49-51. Be sure students understand how to use these three pages.

❀ Point out that on the Pet Idea Web students fill in the cells in response to their labels. They add labels to two cells and then jot down whatever makes sense. On the Pet Picture Page, they may draw their pets, or attach photographs. For this page, explain that a *caption* is a short, descriptive sentence that tells something about a picture or photograph. Students use the Pet Story Form for the final draft of their pet stories.

Write!

❀ Provide a variety of books about pets for students to browse through. Have your school librarian recommend titles about dogs, cats, fish, birds, rabbits, and other pets, such as hamsters, gerbils, mice, snakes, and turtles.

❀ If you have a class pet, you might direct some students to observe it as a living prompt!

Get Together

❀ Group students according to the kind of animal they wrote about. Have them share their writing within their pet interest group.

❀ Challenge students to match descriptions of pets with their pictures.

❀ Extend by having students generate questions about pets. These can become the basis for a research project in which students use library or Internet resources to find the answers. They may also use the questions to interview a veterinarian or pet shop owner.

Quick & Fun Writing Activities Just for Young Learners • Scholastic Professional Books

Name _____

 Is for Pet

Write about your pet here.

My pet's name is _____ .

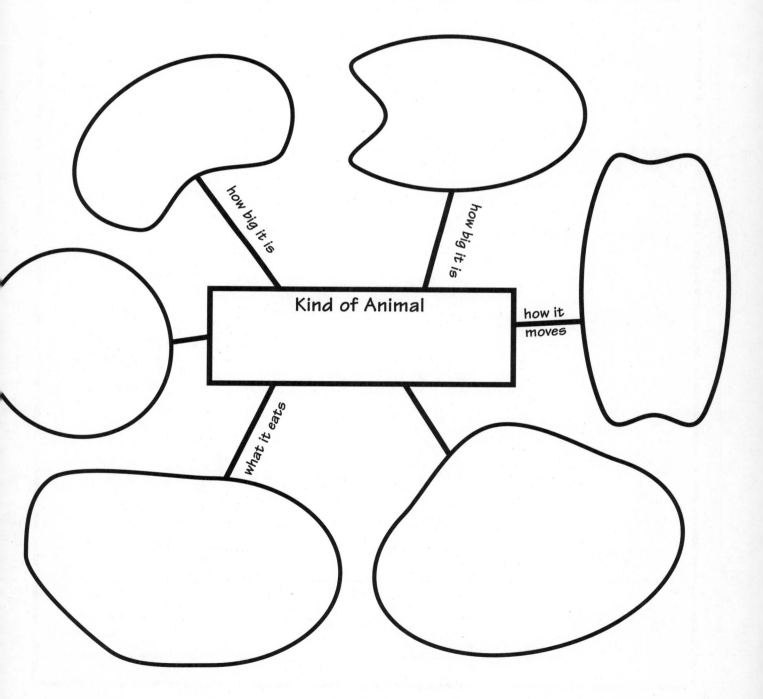

Name _____

P Is for Pet

Draw or glue a picture of your pet below.
Then write a caption for your picture.

Caption:

_____

_____

_____

Quick & Fun Writing Activities Just for Young Learners • Scholastic Professional Books

Name _____

P Is for Pet

Now write a story about your pet.

Quick & Fun Writing Activities Just for Young Learners • Scholastic Professional Books

Ⓠ Is for Quotation

Objective: Pairs of students have dialogues and then record what was said.

▓ Get Ready . . .

❂ Engage students by writing a quotation on the board. You might use words a famous person said, recurring phrases a popular TV character says, or words that someone in the class says. Write it inside quotation marks.

❂ Invite volunteers to demonstrate a *dialogue*, or conversation between two people. Ask students to notice how the remarks go back and forth between the two speakers.

❂ Explain that a *quotation* is the exact words someone says. You can emphasize this by holding big quotation marks around the head of the person who is speaking, and by occasionally asking the class to repeat exactly what the speaker just said.

❂ Display examples of quotations from the newspaper. You can include comic strips, in which the words each character says appear in dialogue bubbles.

▓ Get Set . . .

❂ Tell students that they are going to have a conversation with a partner, and then write down what they said. Duplicate and distribute the Quotation Planner and Dialogue Bubble Form on pages 53-54. Be sure students understand how to use these pages.

❂ Break the class into pairs or quartets to work on this activity.

▓ Write!

❂ Ask pairs (or quartets) to brainstorm topics they might like to talk about. They can jot down their ideas on the Quotation Planner. Once students agree on a topic, have them simply begin to talk in a natural give-and-take fashion. After a few exchanges, ask them to stop and think back on what they said. Partners record what they said on the Dialogue Bubble Form.

❂ Provide extra copies of the Dialogue Bubble Form for longer conversations.

▓ Get Together

❂ Have students exchange Dialogue Bubble Forms. Pairs can take turns acting out the dialogue by reading the quotations aloud. The rest of the class might enjoy trying to guess which pair originated the conversation.

❂ Challenge students to write their own dialogue on a chosen topic. In this instance, each student creates *both* parts of the dialogue. They may use the Dialogue Bubble Sheet.

❂ Extend by asking students to act as reporters, jotting down exact quotations from classmates as you hold a class discussion.

Quick & Fun Writing Activities Just for Young Learners • Scholastic Professional Books

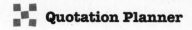

Name _____

Ⓠ Is for Quotation

What shall we talk about?
List some ideas.

Name _____

Q Is for Quotation

Time to talk!

Have a chat. Then write down what you said.

Use the bubbles below.

R Is for Recipe

Objective: Students make up recipes with silly ingredients and provide step-by-step instructions.

Get Ready . . .

❂ Engage students by displaying kids' cookbooks they can browse through. Examples include *Mud Pies and Other Recipes: A Cookbook for Dolls* by Marjorie Winslow, *Pretend Soup and Other Real Recipes* by Mollie Katzen, and *Kids' First Cookbook: Delicious Nutritious Treats to Make Yourself* by The American Cancer Society.

❂ Read aloud these lines from Shakepeare's play, *Macbeth*, in which three witches list some of the ingredients of a secret potion: "Eye of newt and toe of frog/Wool of bat and tongue of dog. . . ." You may also read any version of the famous folktale *Stone Soup*.

❂ Tell students that a *recipe* is a set of instructions for preparing and cooking food. Point out that people follow recipes to know which ingredients to get, which utensils to use, how many servings the recipe will provide, and the sequence of steps to follow.

❂ Invite students to share cooking experiences they have had. Discuss following a recipe.

❂ Display pictures of foods that are easy enough for supervised students to prepare, such as cookies, cupcakes, brownies, pancakes, pretzels, sandwiches, eggs, and soups.

Get Set . . .

❂ Tell students that they are going to make up a recipe for a far-fetched food. Duplicate and distribute the Recipe Forms on pages 56-57. Remind students that these pages go together.

❂ Brainstorm a list of real foods that students like to eat. Then prompt kids' creative juices by suggesting twists on standard fare, such as Pickle Stew, Toothpaste Soup, Mustard Cream Pie, Beggar's Burgers, or Donut Salad.

Write!

❂ Urge students to be creative and silly. Allow them to use outrageous ingredients and far-out cooking techniques.

❂ Despite its inherent humor and fancy, this task requires thought. Students must plan the order of steps, give a complete list of ingredients (with measurements!), and estimate how many servings their concoctions may provide!

❂ Guide students in listing ingredients in the order cooks will use them.

Get Together

❂ Have students collect the recipes into a kooky class cookbook.

❂ Extend by having students write recipes for real, simple, yet edible dishes.

Quick & Fun Writing Activities Just for Young Learners • Scholastic Professional Books

Name _____

R Is for Recipe

A *recipe* is a set of instructions for preparing and cooking food. Create a silly recipe. List the utensils (tools) and ingredients (food) someone will need.

A Yummy Recipe

Recipe Name: _____

It serves _____ people.

Get these utensils (Bowls? Spoons?):

_____   _____

_____   _____

_____   _____

_____   _____

_____   _____

Get these ingredients (Eggs? Dry bread?):

_____   _____

_____   _____

_____   _____

_____   _____

56

Name _____

R Is for Recipe

Now tell how to make the recipe.
Write the steps in order.

A Yummy Recipe

What to do:

1. _____
_____
_____

2. _____
_____
_____

3. _____
_____
_____

4. _____
_____
_____

5. _____
_____

6. _____
_____
_____

S Is for Senses

Objective: Students fill in a sensory details chart about objects and then write descriptions.

Get Ready . . .

❂ Engage students by sharing books about the senses, such as *My Five Senses* by Aliki or *The Five Senses* by Sally Hewitt.

❂ Explain that human beings, like all living creatures, have senses. The senses take in information about the world; then the brain makes sense of it. Our five senses are hearing, seeing, tasting, touching, and smelling.

❂ Draw a 5-column chart. Write each of the five senses at the head of a column. Have students suggest words that relate to each sense. Get them started by listing the words *scent, odor,* and *sniff* with the sense of smell. Record kids' words and ideas.

Get Set . . .

❂ Tell students that they will complete a web about the five senses, and then use the details to write a description of something. Duplicate and distribute the Sense Details Web and Senses Description Form on pages 59-60. Be sure students understand how to use the pages.

❂ Have students select something to use for their sensory observation. It might be a favorite object at home or in the classroom, such as a pet, a plant, a toy or a food. If you prefer, assign a particular object.

Write!

❂ Have students list words or phrases in each of the sense boxes in the web on page 59. These ideas will help them write their descriptions on page 60.

❂ Allow emergent writers to work in pairs or small groups to collaborate on their web and descriptive piece.

Get Together

❂ Have partners exchange descriptions and try to guess each other's object. Then let authors read their descriptions aloud. Talk about the clues that were most helpful.

❂ Challenge students to create Sensory Details Posters. Use five large sheets of paper or poster board. Label each with one of the five senses. Help students add sensory words to the posters. Post them so students can refer to them during any writing activity. Tell students that using good sensory details makes good writing even better.

❂ Extend by having students mask one of their senses (i.e., wear a blindfold or earplugs; hold their noses, and so on) and try to identity something using their other senses.

Quick & Fun Writing Activities Just for Young Learners • Scholastic Professional Books

Name _____

S Is for Senses

Pick an object. Tell about it for each of your five senses.
(*Be careful!* Don't taste anything without asking first!)

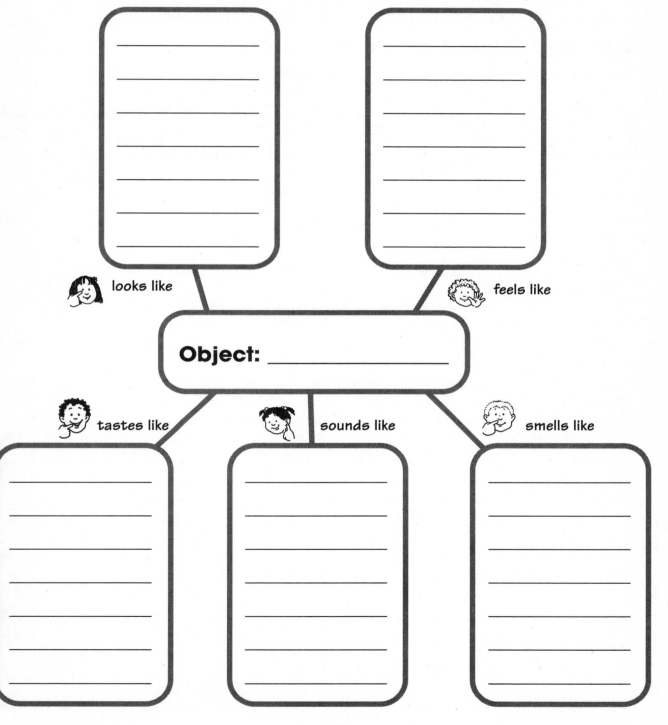

looks like

feels like

Object: _____

tastes like

sounds like

smells like

59

Name _____

S Is for Senses

Can somebody else make sense of *your* senses?

Describe an object, but *don't tell* what it is.

Use lots of sense details.

Then switch papers with a partner.

Can you guess each other's object?

_____

_____

_____

_____

_____

_____

_____

_____

_____

What is it? _____

T Is for Top Ten

Objective: Students create their own top ten countdown lists on topics of their choice.

▦ Get Ready . . .

❂ Display pictures of events that are associated with countdowns, such as a rocket launch, the implosion of a building, the start of a race, or the final seconds of a sporting event.

❂ Engage students by having the class count down from 10 to 1. For older students, try counting backwards from 100 to 1.

❂ Present a Top Ten list you might find in a children's magazine, or one you make up in advance. Point out that the list has a theme or topic, and that all its items fit the topic. Following the adage "Save the best for last," the author of the list arranges the items in order from good to better to best; the most exciting entry is given last.

❂ Brainstorm a list of topics for which students might create Top Ten lists. Some ideas include the following: The Top Ten After-School Plans, The Top Ten Party Ideas, The Top Ten Vacation Spots, The Top Ten Snack Foods, The Top Ten Pets, The Top Ten Athletes, The Top Ten Funny Words, The Top Ten Reasons Why _____, The Top Ten Excuses for Not _____, The Top Ten Answers to _____, The Top Ten Ways to _____, and so on.

▦ Get Set . . .

❂ Tell students that they are going to create their own Top Ten lists. Duplicate and distribute the Top Ten Countdown Form on page 62. Be sure students understand how to use the page.

❂ You may want to assign a particular topic to your students, or you may prefer to have them select their own. Students can work individually, in pairs, or in small groups.

▦ Write!

❂ Suggest that students start with a first-draft list, which need *not* be in the best order. Once they have ten items, they can rearrange the order so that the best is last (as #1).

❂ Discuss sensible ways to rearrange the items. One way is for kids to write items on index cards. They can then spread out the cards on their desks or tables and physically put the cards into the order they like best.

▦ Get Together

❂ Have students read their lists—in dramatic fashion—to the class or small groups.

❂ Challenge students to explain why the items on their lists appear in the order they do.

❂ Extend by having students make Top Ten lists across the curriculum. For instance, they might list the Top Ten Cities in your state in population order, or they might list the Top Ten books the class would recommend for summer reading.

Quick & Fun Writing Activities Just for Young Learners • Scholastic Professional Books

Name _____

𝕋 Is for Top Ten

Make a Top Ten list. Save the best for last!

The Top Ten

_____

_____

10. _____

9. _____

8. _____

7. _____

6. _____

5. _____

4. _____

3. _____

2. _____

And now—the Number 1 item is . . .

1. _____

62

U Is for Under

Objective: Students write about what it might be like being under the water or under the earth.

Get Ready . . .

- Engage students by sharing books about the lives of creatures that live under the sea or under the ground, or about people, real or imagined, who visit these environments. Titles include *Exploring the Deep, Dark Sea* by Gail Gibbons, *The Great Undersea Search* by Kate Needham, and *Under the Ground* by Claude Delafosse.

- Play and sing the song "Under the Sea," from the animated film *The Little Mermaid*.

- Post pictures of undersea, underwater, or underground life. Ask students to imagine what life might be like in such places. Talk about the special features or habits that plants and animals have that allow them to survive under water or under the earth.

- Display pictures of assorted tools or equipment used to explore underground or underwater locations. These might include flashlights, scuba gear, lighted hard-hats, shovels, rope, gloves, cameras, diving bells, and so on.

Get Set . . .

- Tell students they are going to think about what it might be like to live, work, or visit a place that is under water or under the earth, and then write a story about it. Students can approach this in two ways: they can pretend to be a creature that does live in one of these environments, or they can pretend to be temporary visitors—scientists, explorers, or adventurers.

- Duplicate and distribute the Under the Land and Under Water Environment Forms on pages 64-65, and the Under . . . Stationery on page 66. Make sure students understand how to use these pages.

Write!

- Have students gather words and ideas on the Environment Forms before they begin to draft a story on the Under . . . Stationery.

- It may help spark students' imaginations if they work with partners or in small groups. They can talk together as they formulate their ideas.

Get Together

- Have students share their Under . . . stories to the class or with small groups. Collect the completed stories in two binders, one for each environment.

- Challenge students to revise their stories to include more sensory details. They might complete a Senses Details Web (page 59) to help them accomplish this revision.

- Extend by having students write poems about their special environment. You can also invite people who have gone scuba diving, been in a submarine, or have explored an underground cave to share their experiences with the class.

Name _____

U Is for Under

Here is an underground scene.
List some words that fit this environment.

Name _____

U Is for Under

Here is an underwater scene.
List some words that fit this environment.

Quick & Fun Writing Activities Just for Young Learners • Scholastic Professional Books

Name _____

U Is for Under

Think about living underground or underwater.
Then write about living under the surface.

Quick & Fun Writing Activities Just for Young Learners • Scholastic Professional Books

V Is for Valentine

Objective: Students create personalized Valentine's Day cards.

Get Ready . . .

❂ Engage students by sharing books about love, such as *Love and Kisses* by Sarah Wilson, *Somebody Loves You, Mr. Hatch* by Eileen Spinelli, or *A Village Full of Valentines* by James Stevenson.

❂ Sing or play songs about love, such as "Love Is Something If You Give It Away" or "I Love You a Bushel and a Peck," as well as popular songs and folk tunes that students know.

❂ Display a variety of Valentine's Day cards, both commercial and homemade. Ask students to identify the ones they like best and tell why.

❂ Brainstorm with students to find ways to finish the following statement: "Love is . . ." They might say things like "Love is feeling safe and happy," or "Love is how I feel about my mom."

Get Set . . .

❂ Tell students that they are going to write a special valentine to someone they care about. Duplicate and distribute the Divine Valentine Form on page 68. Be sure students understand how to use it. You may want to prepare additional copies for students who would like to make more than one valentine.

❂ Suggest that a valentine can be a poem, song lyrics, a love letter, or simply a heartfelt statement that would please the person receiving it.

❂ Be prepared to help students decide whom to make a valentine for—a family member, friend, teacher, pet, fictional character, or famous person.

Write!

❂ Have students write first drafts on ordinary paper. Then they can copy their final drafts onto the Divine Valentine Form.

❂ Encourage students to add artistic or decorative touches to their valentines.

Get Together

❂ Have students share their valentine cards, or provide envelopes they can use to send their valentines.

❂ Challenge students to create the perfect valentine they'd like to get from someone!

❂ Extend by having students write about favorite Valentine's Day memories.

Quick & Fun Writing Activities Just for Young Learners • Scholastic Professional Books

Name _____

V Is for Valentine

Make a divine valentine for someone you love.

W Is for Weather

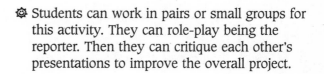

Objective: Students plan mock weather reports to present orally.

Get Ready . . .

❂ Engage students by sharing books about the weather and weather forecasting, such as *What Will the Weather Be?* by Lynda Dewitt, *What Makes the Weather* by Janet Palazzo, or *How's the Weather?* by Melvin Berger.

❂ Play or sing songs about weather conditions. Sing "It's Raining, It's Pouring" or "You Are My Sunshine."

❂ Display or create a set of simple icons to suggest a variety of weather conditions, such as a cloud for cloudy, an umbrella for rain, a snowflake for snow, and so on. Many commercially-available classroom calendars provide such icons.

❂ Talk with the class about television weather broadcasts they have seen. Then tape several weather reports from local stations and show them to the class. Compare and contrast the style of the broadcasters, the content of the report, the order in which information is given, the weather graphics, and so on.

Get Set . . .

❂ Tell students that they are going to plan and present a mock weather report, as if they were on television. Duplicate and distribute the Weather Picture, Weather Words, and Weather Reporter's Forms on pages 70-72. Be sure students understand how to use these pages.

❂ Students can work in pairs or small groups for this activity. They can role-play being the reporter. Then they can critique each other's presentations to improve the overall project.

Write!

❂ Provide weather maps from daily newspapers, or help students locate weather Web sites where they can get accurate information to use in their mock reports.

❂ Remind students that weather reports are usually cheery and friendly. Point out that even when weather conditions may be serious, broadcasters usually stay calm and comforting. Encourage students to use a friendly, informal style.

Get Together

❂ Have groups take turns presenting their reports. If possible, videotape them.

❂ Challenge students to analyze the reports that classmates gave. Which ones were the most helpful? Which were the most accurate-sounding? Which were the most original?

❂ Extend by connecting this activity with a science unit on weather. Students can research different kinds of weather conditions—the water cycle, clouds, and so on. Link with math by helping students graph daily temperature highs and lows, sunrise and sunset times, and so on.

Name _____

W **Is for Weather**

Draw a picture of the weather.

70

Name _____

W Is for Weather

Here are some weather words to use.

HOT DAYS

broiling	muggy
hazy	shade
sweltering	summer
humid	steamy

STORMY DAYS

lightning	storm
pouring	thunder
rain	drizzle
showers	downpour

WINTER DAYS

freezing	sleet
frosty	snow
frozen	frigid
icy	slick

CLOUDY DAYS

clearing	overcast
cloudy	partly
foggy	cloudy
gray	skies

NICE DAYS

beautiful	fresh
clear	sunny
comfortable	warm
crisp	cool

OTHER WORDS

conditions	tomorrow
forecast	yesterday
predict	fall
radar	spring
today	change

71

Name _____

W Is for Weather

Write down things to say in your weather report.

 **Is for X-Ray**

Objective: Students imagine what they could see inside the body thanks to X-ray technology.

Get Ready . . .

❂ Engage students by sharing books about X-rays, such as *Bones* by Stephen Krensky, or *The Mysterious Rays of Dr. Rontgen* by Beverly Gherman.

❂ Display actual X-rays so students can see what they look like. Contact the school nurse or a local clinic, dental office, or radiology office for assistance. Invite students who have had X-rays taken to share their experiences.

❂ Explain that today there are other ways, besides using X-rays, to look inside the body. These include the sonogram, CAT scan, and MRI (magnetic resonance imaging). These technologies rely on computers to recreate images using sound, magnetic waves, and other kinds of high-tech methods. They can show soft tissues as well as bones. Display examples of sonograms, CAT scans, and MRIs, if possible.

Get Set . . .

❂ Tell students that they are going to pretend that they can see inside the body and then write about what they imagine. Duplicate and distribute the X-Ray Questions on pages 74-75. Be sure students understand how to use these pages.

Write!

❂ To stimulate students' curiosity, invite them to talk to each other as they list their ideas.

❂ Students may use another sheet of paper to complete the X-Ray Questions Form on page 74.

❂ Allow emergent writers to work with more advanced partners who can help them plan and write.

Get Together

❂ Have students read aloud their responses to selected X-ray questions.

❂ Challenge students to try to identify the parts of the body they see in actual X-ray images.

❂ Extend by helping students do research to learn more about what is inside the body. You might invite the school nurse, a radiology technician, or a doctor to speak to the class and to bring in models and graphics to stimulate discussion.

Quick & Fun Writing Activities Just for Young Learners • Scholastic Professional Books

Name _____

Is for X-Ray

X-rays let doctors look inside bodies.

If you could look inside the body, where would you want to look?

_____

_____

_____

What would you want to see?

_____

_____

_____

How do you think it might look?

_____

_____

_____

How can X-rays help doctors help people?

_____

_____

_____

Did you ever have an X-ray or other test for looking inside your body? Tell about it.

_____

_____

_____

Quick & Fun Writing Activities Just for Young Learners • Scholastic Professional Books

Name _____

X Is for X-Ray

Suppose you could know more about how your body works. What would you want to know? Think about it!

I would like to know more about _____

_____

_____

_____

_____

I am curious because _____

_____

_____

_____

Here are some questions I would ask: _____

_____

_____

_____

_____

_____

Quick & Fun Writing Activities Just for Young Learners • Scholastic Professional Books

Y Is for Yellow

Objective: Students write color descriptions and list things that share a common color.

Get Ready . . .

❂ Engage students by sharing books about colors, such as *Color* by Ruth Heller, *Chidi Only Likes Blue: An African Book of Colors* by Ifeoma Onyefulu, *Color Dance* by Ann Jonas, *Colors* by Ken Nordine, or *The Crayon Box That Talked* by Shane Derolf.

❂ Create a cheerful bulletin board display arranged by color. Invite students to cut out pictures of things for each color and add them to the display in the appropriate region.

❂ Explain that some colors can be associated with particular feelings. For example, they may know that *feeling blue* means feeling sad or gloomy. Talk about the kinds of feelings we associate with different colors.

Get Set . . .

❂ Tell students that they are going to create a list of descriptions that go with certain colors, as well as a list of things that usually are that color. Duplicate and distribute the Color Collection Forms on pages 77–78. Be sure students understand how to use the pages.

❂ Help students get started by offering them some examples. For instance, you might say that "Yellow is *sunny, bright, cheerful, buttery* . . ." or "These are yellow things—*bananas, suns, lemons, baby chicks* . . ."

Write!

❂ As students write, play songs whose titles contain color words, such as "Yellow Submarine," "Blue Moon," or "It's Not Easy Being Green."

❂ Jazz up this task by providing colored pencils or markers for students to use.

❂ Allow students to browse through magazines, books, catalogs, and other media to find examples of objects that customarily come in certain colors.

Get Together

❂ Have students display their completed Color Collection Forms.

❂ Challenge students to write a creative description of something *not* in its characteristic color, such as a blue banana, an orange sky, or a pink frog.

❂ Extend by having students make rainbow paintings, banners, or posters to hang around the room on a dreary day. Conclude by having students write color poems in this format: Red is _____, Blue is _____, Green is _____, and so on.

Quick & Fun Writing Activities Just for Young Learners • Scholastic Professional Books

Name _____

Y Is for Yellow

Tell about nine colors.
Write words that describe each color.
Name things that come in each color.

Yellow is _____.

These are <u>yellow</u> things: _____

_____

Green is _____.

These are <u>green</u> things: _____

_____

Blue is _____.

These are <u>blue</u> things: _____

_____

Purple is _____.

These are <u>purple</u> things: _____

_____

Quick & Fun Writing Activities Just for Young Learners • Scholastic Professional Books

Name _____

Y Is for Yellow

Red is _____.

These are red things: _____

_____.

Orange is _____.

These are orange things: _____

_____.

Brown is _____.

These are brown things: _____

_____.

Black is _____.

These are black things: _____

_____.

White is _____.

These are white things: _____

_____.

Z Is for Zoo

Objective: *Students write informative signs that might be posted in a zoo.*

◾ Get Ready . . .

- ✿ Engage students by sharing books about zoos, such as *My Visit to the Zoo* by Aliki, or *The Tiger Has a Toothache* by Patricia Lauber.

- ✿ Sing songs about zoo animals, such as the old favorites "I Went to the Animal Fair," or "Going to the Zoo" by Tom Paxton.

- ✿ Display pictures of zoo animals, zoo habitats, zoo workers, zoo posters, and so on. Focus on the different ways that visitors can get information about the animals—from signs; from drawings, maps, and charts; by asking zoo workers; or by watching filmstrips or videotapes.

- ✿ Talk about the kinds of information people may want when they visit a zoo. Discuss the kinds of facts that would interest them, such as where an animal lives in the wild, how big (or small) it is, what it eats, how it hunts, how it cares for its young, and so on.

◾ Get Set . . .

- ✿ Tell students that they are going to prepare a helpful sign for a zoo animal of their choice. Duplicate and distribute the Zoo Facts Forms on pages 80-81. Be sure students understand how to use these pages.

- ✿ If you prefer, assign a particular zoo animal to each student or pair.

◾ Write!

- ✿ Have students work in pairs. Invite partners to ask each other questions about their chosen (or assigned) animals. This can guide their research and writing.

- ✿ Encourage artistic learners or mathematical learners to include drawings, maps, or graphs of pertinent information about their animals.

◾ Get Together

- ✿ Have students display their Zoo Facts Forms with photos or drawings of their animals.

- ✿ Challenge students to share key facts from their Zoo Facts Forms without naming the animal. Classmates can try to guess each animal based on the details presented.

- ✿ Extend by having students do more comprehensive animal research projects. To accompany written reports or fact sheets, they can make clay models of their animals, and provide maps that show where the animals are found in the wild.

Quick & Fun Writing Activities Just for Young Learners • Scholastic Professional Books

Name _____

Z **Is for Zoo**

Pick a zoo animal. Tell about it.

My zoo animal is the _____.

This animal is a kind of _____.

In the wild, this animal lives in _____.

Usually, the color(s) of this animal_____.

It is about the size of _____.

Its body is covered with _____.

It eats _____.

It moves by _____.

It makes this sound: _____.

When it is born, it _____

_____.

If I ever saw one up close, I would _____

_____

_____

Name _____

Z Is for Zoo

List some ideas to help you
find out about your zoo animal.

My zoo animal is the _____ .

Some books I can use for facts: _____

_____

_____

Some Web sites I can visit for facts: _____

_____

_____

Some cool facts about my zoo animal: _____

_____

_____

Here is a picture of my animal:

_____

81

Appendix

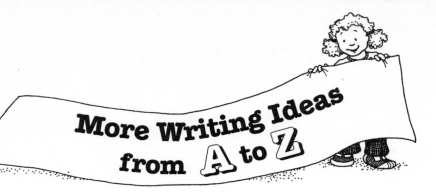

More Writing Ideas from A to Z

A
Animal Descriptions
Advice Letter
Adopt a Pet Ad
Architecture Review

B
Book Blurb
Baby-Sitter Notes
Birthday Wishes
Beyond the Horizon Poem

C
Commercial
Clothing Description
Character Sketch
Comic Book Story

D
Dear Diary
Dialogue
Danger Warning Notice
Doodle
Description

E
Excellent Adventures
Explorer's Notebook
Elephant's Shopping List
Engine Explanation

F
Fairy Tales
Favorites List
Fabulous Foods
Following Directions

G
Guest Rules
Gadget Description
Grandparent Letter
Games Instructions

H
Holiday Memories
How-to Description
Happy-Gram
Historical Fiction

I
Invitation
Invention Description
Instruction Manual
Impress Your Friends!

J
Jar of Wishes
Jealousy Poem
Jungle Sounds Story
Jingle Lyrics

K
Write what you KNOW!
Kitchen Description
Kid's Day Celebration!
King's Castle Story

L
Lyrics
Lists
Love Letters
Lost-and-Found Descriptions

M

Messages (phone machine, e-mail)
Musical Instruments
Behind a **M**ask
Million Kid March

N

Notes
New Experiences
News Reports
How I Got a **N**ickname

O

One Great Wish
Outer Space
Observation Report
The **O**ldest Person I Know

P

Poems
Predictions
The **P**lot Thickens!
Prescription for Fun

Q

Questions to an Author
Quiet Is _____
Quick Write
My Best **Q**ualities

R

Riddles
Remembering _____
Robot to the **R**escue!
Rhyme Time

S

Setting the **S**tage
Sales Pitch
Safety Rules
Silly **S**andwiches

T

Tall **T**ales
Travel Writing
For the **T**ime Capsule
Tongue **T**wisters

U

Unusual Endings
Umbrella Poem
Unicorn (describe fanciful animals)
Unbelievable!

V

Viewing a **V**olcano!
Victory Speech
The **V**acant Lot
Tasty Ways to Serve **V**egetables

W

Wish List
In the **W**aiting Room
Excuse Me, **W**aiter!
Weird Experiences

X

X Marks the Spot
Xylophones and Other Instruments
Xylem and Phloem (Inside a Tree)

Y

My Favorite Time of **Y**ear
In Our **Y**ard
The Huge **Y**awn
When I Was **Y**ounger

Z

ZIP Code (describe where you live)
If I had a **Z**illion _____
Zebras Have Stripes
Zero Means _____

Self-Evaluation Checklist

☐ Did I say what I wanted to say?

☐ Can others understand what I mean?

☐ Did I give enough facts and details?

☐ Did I leave out any words or ideas?

☐ Do I want to add anything?

☐ Is my piece in order? Does it have a beginning, a middle, and an end?

☐ Could I use some better words?

☐ Does each sentence start with a capital letter?

☐ Do I have end punctuation marks?

☐ Did I check spelling?

☐ Did I write a title?

☐ Did I read my work out loud to hear how it sounds?

Other comments: _____

_____

_____

_____

_____

_____

Quick & Fun Writing Activities Just for Young Learners • Scholastic Professional Books

Editor's Marks

Begin a new paragraph here.   ¶

Make a capital letter.   it

Add a word here.   the ʌ car
                                                 red

Take out a word.   after that lunch

Add a period.   Dr⊙ Wong
                                                  ʌ

Add a question mark.   May I go ?
                                                        ∨

Check the spelling.   mothir (sp)

Does this sound right?   baby tooths (k?)

Sample Edited Paragraph

¶ Last Thursday, we went to the dentist. I had my first loose tooth. it wiggled back and forth.

First, we went to lunch. We parked next to a red car. I ate a tuna sandwich. I chewed very carefully because my tooth was so loose. After that lunch, I brushed each tooth very carefully, too. Then we went to see Dr. Wong, who is the best dentist in the world.

"I want to go in to see Dr. Wong by myself. May I go?" I asked my mothir. (SP) She smiled and nodded.

I hopped into the chair and opened my mouth wide. "Look, Dr. Wong!" I wiggled my loose tooth back and forth. "I'm about to lose one of my baby tooths!" (k?)

Quick & Fun Writing Activities Just for Young Learners • Scholastic Professional Books

Certificate of Merit
for
Growth in Writing

is given to

for

Teacher

Date

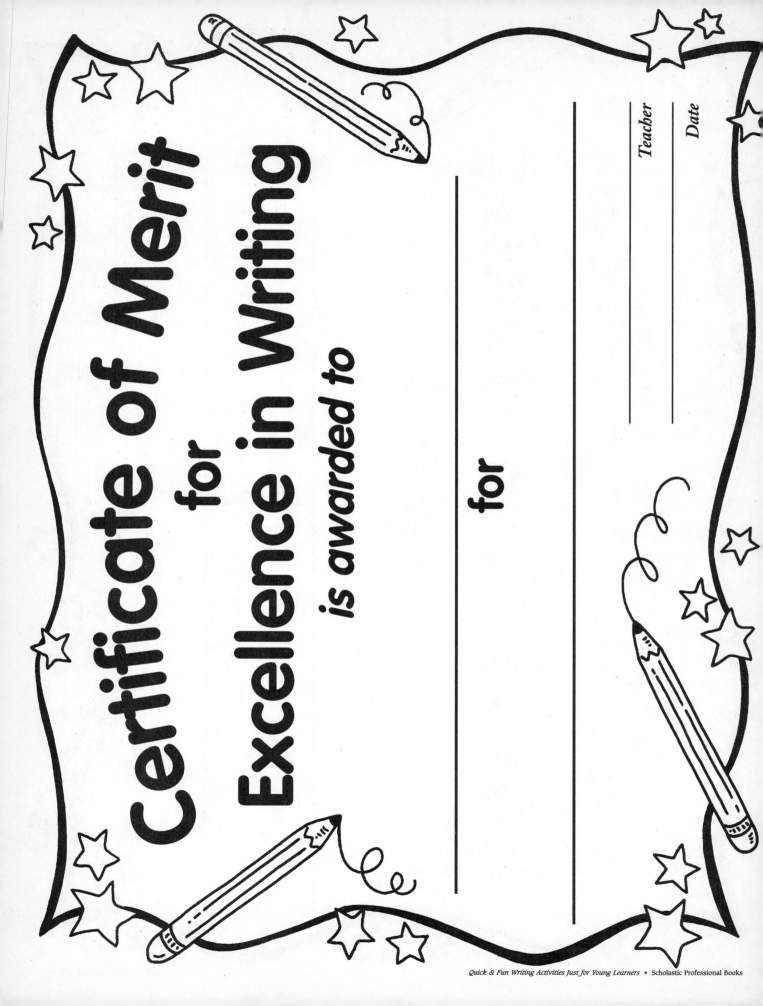

Certificate of Merit
for
Excellence in Writing

is awarded to

for

Teacher

Date

Certificate of Merit

for

Originality in Writing

is presented to

for

Teacher

Date

Author's Award

is hereby presented to

to honor OUTSTANDING

Teacher

Date

Notes

Notes

Notes

Notes